SPALDING GRAY:
Stories Left to Tell

Words by Spalding Gray
Concept by Kathleen Russo and Lucy Sexton

Dramatic Publishing
Woodstock, Illinois • England • Australia • New Zealand

*** NOTICE ***

The amateur and stock acting rights to this work are controlled exclusively by THE DRAMATIC PUBLISHING COMPANY without whose permission in writing no performance of it may be given. Royalty must be paid every time a play is performed whether or not it is presented for profit and whether or not admission is charged. A play is performed any time it is acted before an audience. Current royalty rates, applications and restrictions may be found at our Web site: www.dramaticpublishing.com, or we may be contacted by mail at: DRAMATIC PUBLISHING COMPANY, 311 Washington St., Woodstock IL 60098.

COPYRIGHT LAW GIVES THE AUTHOR OR THE AUTHOR'S AGENT THE EXCLUSIVE RIGHT TO MAKE COPIES. This law provides authors with a fair return for their creative efforts. Authors earn their living from the royalties they receive from book sales and from the performance of their work. Conscientious observance of copyright law is not only ethical, it encourages authors to continue their creative work. This work is fully protected by copyright. No alterations, deletions or substitutions may be made in the work without the prior written consent of the publisher. No part of this work may be reproduced or transmitted in any form or by any means, electronic or mechanical, including photocopy, recording, videotape, film, or any information storage and retrieval system, without permission in writing from the publisher. It may not be performed either by professionals or amateurs without payment of royalty. All rights, including, but not limited to, the professional, motion picture, radio, television, videotape, foreign language, tabloid, recitation, lecturing, publication and reading, are reserved.

For performance of any songs, music and recordings mentioned in this play which are in copyright, the permission of the copyright owners must be obtained or other songs and recordings in the public domain substituted.

©MMVIII by
SPALDING GRAY

Printed in the United States of America
All Rights Reserved
(SPALDING GRAY: STORIES LEFT TO TELL)

ISBN: 978-1-58342-560-2

IMPORTANT BILLING AND CREDIT REQUIREMENTS

All producers of the play *must* give credit to the author and conceivers of the play in all programs distributed in connection with performances of the play and in all instances in which the title of the play appears for purposes of advertising, publicizing or otherwise exploiting the play and/or a production. The name of the author *must* also appear on a separate line, on which no other name appears, immediately following the title, and the names of both conceivers *must* also appear on a separate line immediately following the author's credit, and the names of author and conceivers *must* appear in size of type not less than fifty percent (50%) the size of the title type. Biographical information on the author and conceivers, if included in the playbook, may be used in all programs. Author and conceivers must be credited as follows: "Words by Spalding Gray, Concept by Kathleen Russo and Lucy Sexton." All producers of the play *must* include the following announcement on the title page of all programs distributed in connection with performances of the play and in advertising and publicity for the play wherever and whenever all production credits appear: "*Spalding Gray: Stories Left to Tell* was originally produced in New York by Eric Falkenstein, Michael Alden and Naked Angels (Jenny Gersten, Artistic Director) in association with Judith Ann Abrams, Jamie DeRoy and Mort Swinsky." *In all programs this notice must appear:*

"Produced by special arrangement with
THE DRAMATIC PUBLISHING COMPANY of Woodstock, Illinois"

Spalding Gray: Stories Left to Tell is created entirely from Spalding Gray's own words, except for a letter from Rockwell Gray to Spalding Gray dated December 8, 1966, used by permission of its author. In addition to journal extracts and other unpublished writing, *Stories Left to Tell* includes excerpts from the following works by Spalding Gray: *Sex and Death to the Age of 14; Terrors of Pleasure; Swimming to Cambodia; Impossible Vacation; Gray's Anatomy; Monster in a Box; It's a Slippery Slope; Morning, Noon and Night* and *Life Interrupted.*

Spalding Gray: Stories Left to Tell by Spalding Gray was originally produced in New York by Eric Falkenstein, Michael Alden and Naked Angels (Jenny Gersten, artistic director) in association with Judith Ann Abrams, Jamie DeRoy and Mort Swinsky at the Minetta Lane Theatre, with an opening-night performance on March 6, 2007. It was conceived by Kathleen Russo and directed by Lucy Sexton, with set design by David Korins, costume design by Michael Krass, lighting design by Ben Stanton, original music and sound design by Fitz Patton, productions by Leah Gelpe, production management by Shannon Nicole Case, production stage management by Matthew Silver, casting by Hopkins, Smith & Barden, press representation by Sacks & Co., and general management by Richards/Climan, Inc. The cast on opening night consisted of Fisher Stevens in the guest performer role of Career, and Kathleen Chalfant, Hazelle Goodman, Ain Gordon and Frank Wood in the ensemble roles of Love, Adventure, Journals and Family, respectively.

Spalding Gray: Stories Left to Tell was originally created and developed in association with Washington Square Arts under the title *Leftover Stories to Tell*.

Author's Notes

Stories Left to Tell came about when Theatre Communications Group republished *Swimming to Cambodia* in May 2004. TCG held a reading for the book's release at the Union Square Barnes & Noble where Roger Rosenblatt, Reno, Kate Valk, Eric Bogosian and Bob Holman all read excerpts. It was a "light-bulb moment" for me as I sat there listening to all these other voices read Spalding's work and receiving an enthusiastic response from the audience. That night made me realize more than ever that Spalding was a brilliant writer. His words, not his own performance, were now taking center stage.

Spalding would have been 65 on June 5, 2006. "In honor of his birthday, I began planning a celebration reading of his work for around that time at Performance Space 122, where a workshop version of the show, entitled *Leftover Stories to Tell*, received its premiere. When UCLA heard about it, they also booked it for a week in June. We even got the mayor to proclaim June 5th Spalding Gray Day in New York City.

I thought Lucy Sexton would be a good person to help me organize the actors and publicity for the event. At our first meeting, Lucy had all these great ideas and I realized that maybe we could make this into something more than a reading. Maybe we could make it into a fully staged play and through his writing tell the story of his life, a tribute to the brilliant man I loved, and a vehicle for his work to live on.

— Kathleen Russo

SPALDING GRAY:
Stories Left to Tell

Players: Love, Journals, Family, Adventure, Career

Note: These titles describe the theme of the stories the player reads and performs rather than the "character" portrayed. The performers remain themselves, telling the stories as if they were their own. When not speaking, they watch and listen to the other performers tell their stories; their demeanor is relaxed, collegial and responsive.

Time: The stories are written over the years 1963 to 2003, but the emphasis is on storytelling which always happens in the present place and time.

Setting: The stage setting is simple, using the elements that Spalding himself used in performance: desk, microphone, notebook, glass of water, tape player. As there is more than one person delivering Spalding's stories, the elements are expanded to encompass them. There is one simple table/desk that Journals sits at. The rest of the stage consists of a multi-leveled platform built of wood similar to the desk so the entire playing area becomes a sort of exploded desk. Except for Journals, the other players move about the space as the stories require. There is a wired tabletop mike on the desk as well as mikes on stands around the stage and wireless mikes as needed, so every story is spoken through a microphone. There are notebooks piled around the stage and journal pages hang to create the backdrop. The performers will use these notebooks throughout the show, occasionally actually reading from them but most times using them as a reference point as they tell the stories off book in direct address to the audience. Journals maintains the closest connection to the books, sitting at the desk with an open book throughout the show. (However, Journals also speaks off book as much as possible in order again to be able to speak directly to the audience.) The notebooks simply make it clear the stories spring from the voluminous pages of Spalding's writing, that they are literally the stories he left to tell.

Sound: In addition to the popular music sound cues appearing in the script, an original score can be used to provide transitions between the stories. The interstitial music should have its own voice and thru line in the piece. The stories can also be performed without the interstitial score, but with simply the three pop music cues.

(Performers enter to the Spice Girls "Wannabe." They move notebooks from the desk to the various playing spaces. LOVE opens one of the notebooks and prepares to read. Music fades.)

LOVE

I wake and look out the window, scanning the historic cemetery across the street, where I see the first of the sun's rose-colored light. My eye scans back and goes to Theo, my nine-month old infant son, sleeping beside me. Behind him I see Kathie, his mother, and I think how did I get here? Never in my wildest soothsayer-fantasy-fortuneteller imagination dreams did I think at age fifty-six that I would recreate my original family structure of two adults and three children. Kathie, me, her daughter Marissa, our son Forrest, and our new little Theo.

Kathie always said that even in high school she knew she was going to have three children. What did I know I wanted in high school? What did I know I wanted now?

I get up and call out to Forrest, "What do you want for breakfast, sweetie?"

Cap'n Crunch, he yells back.

I grab Theo and head downstairs. Then Kathie yells to me, "Spalding, please go to the cellar and get Forrest's jeans. They're hanging on the drying rack."

While fumbling around in the basement I hear that some-one named Marissa has put on the Spice Girls' CD. She's playing "Wannabe" top-blast. I am outraged. I feel like I'm living under a disco. I yell "Shut that damn thing down!" Then from the cellar, I hear a big crash of glass and then silence. Then, I hear Forrest call down to me, "Dad, you know that picture of George Washington on his deathbed? Well, he's dead."

Totally exasperated, Kathie yells, "Help me get Marissa out of here."

It's a mad scramble, as if everyone is running to get off a sinking ship. Kathie finishes vacuuming the glass, grabs Marissa, grabs Marissa's knapsack, lunch and sweater and she's out the door and gone.

I am left with the boys. The house is now two people calmer. I take Theo out of the highchair and, lifting him up in my arms, I am suddenly still and at peace. Oh, the blessed weight of a child, of this child. The way he cuddles and fits into my body like a part of me. At that moment I think the world is doomed to overpopulation. No wonder people keep having babies, just to keep holding them.

JOURNALS

Journal entry: The furthest back that I can remember is Mom feeding me in my wooden highchair. When I wouldn't eat she'd start rapping out the opening to Beethoven's 5th symphony. "Da, Da, Dada," and say "that's fate knocking." Now, I wouldn't say that's exactly a performance but it was something more abstract than "eat your food dear" or "think of the starving Koreans" which was, in fact, a line my mother used to incorporate around the time of the Korean war. I still think of it.

It was always hard to imagine those starving Koreans, and even harder now that there are Korean delis on every corner.

ADVENTURE

I was bored with life. I know I shouldn't have been, I know I should be thankful, but it was flat. It was just a flat thing. And I would keep hyping it up with this kind of acting out.

For instance, 4th of July, some fireworks go off outside. I'm just a kid. The little ladyfingers go pop pop pop pop pop pop. I run to the window, and say "Mom! Come quick! Russ Jaman, our neighbor, is up on the roof shooting his kids!" Now this was in the old days, when that wasn't done so often. And my mother would rush to the window, believing it, and then she would go, "Oh Spuddy dear, NO, no no. Now WHY do you have to do this?"

FAMILY

My first pet was a cocker spaniel. Jill. Jealous Jill. We called her that because she was very jealous when my little brother Chan was born. My mother told me that I stopped talking for a long time after Jill died. She said they were thinking of taking me to a psychiatrist, but I don't know where they were going to find a psychiatrist in Barrington, Rhode Island, in 1946. Maybe they were thinking of Providence.

LOVE

In seventh grade I fell in love with Julie Brooks, and Julie Brooks I can only describe as an angel—very full lips, olive skin, long brown hair.

Julie and I and a bunch of us who were hanging out together would have kissing contests. We would all get together and see how long two people could hold a kiss. Someone would time it while the rest of us stood around watching, smoking Lucky Strike Regulars. Julie and I used to kiss for about twenty minutes, just holding our lips pressed tight with no movement at all. I was very uncomfortable because it was hard to breathe.

The other thing we'd do is have make-out sessions in Julie's house when her mother wasn't there, playing "Sha-Boom Sha-Boom" on her little automatic 45-record player.

Then we got into dry humping in the field behind Julie's house in September in the sun. I always liked it in the sun. Six of us would go out there, three boys and three girls, and we'd make different spots in the grass and make out. Julie was always wearing those madras Bermuda shorts that were so popular in the late fifties, and I would get my hand up on her right thigh, and that was enough. I'd never go any further, in my mind, the rest was a jungle.

Once I did touch the jungle, briefly, and I told my friend Ryan Ryder about it. He said, "What, you touched the place she pees out of?" That brought me down and fast. I think he was jealous, but I didn't know about jealousy then. So I went back to keeping my hand on her thigh, dry humping until I would come. I would come in my jeans and then we would go have vanilla Cokes. I was happy and I thought she was happy, too; things were going fine until one of the girls, Linda Chipperfield, asked her mother if she could get pregnant through her clothes, and we never saw Linda again. I think her mother kept her in forever.

JOURNALS

Journal entry 1963: You know I've never told anyone this but the first time I ate a woman out I pulled all the muscles in the back of my neck and thought it was a brain tumor so I went to Mass General, then to a psychiatrist. He listened to me talk for about twenty minutes, then he stopped me and told me I was an existential garbage pail. I think that actually cured me, at least for a while.

FAMILY

That summer the bay was clear, with no algae. We could see all the way down to the bottom as we swam, and Mom and I would swim together.

If I couldn't see everywhere, in all directions at once, which was of course impossible, I would go into a sort of panic. She was a good, relaxed swimmer, as if she belonged to the bay. Mom never noticed my panic. She swam, strong and fearless, ahead of me.

Then we'd dry off in the sun and eat lunch together side by side. Mom always had something simple for lunch, like a glass of milk and a tuna fish sandwich on Pepperidge Farm white bread.

But I really wanted to fly the nest; a big part of me wanted to get out of there. I wanted so to go to Bali, or at least to Provincetown. I wanted to go to Provincetown and—I don't know, get in trouble—maybe even fall in love, whatever that was. I needed to get away from Mom. It was too sticky and warm to be right.

So in the morning I'd load up Mom's big tin-breadbox Ford with all the goodies I felt I needed to survive on the beach in Provincetown: LL Bean sleeping bag, Mom's Metrecal and Instant Breakfast. I'd go say goodbye to Mom and head out for Provincetown. A few blocks from home I'd end up turning around and heading back, unloading the car, and swimming and eating lunch with Mom on the lawn. One last swim, one last lunch.

The next day I'd load up the car again with my sleeping bag, and Mom's Metrecal and Instant Breakfast, and drive a few miles farther and then just end up turning around and coming back. Mom never asked me why I kept coming back. We'd just swim and eat lunch together and sit there on the edge of Narragansett Bay. I never made it to Provincetown that summer.

JOURNALS
September 28, 1965: Dear Rocky, So much has happened and yet so little. I am sitting here looking out my window

at a meaningless gazebo in a meaningless park in this little town in upstate New York. I have for some reason moved to Saratoga Springs. Somewhere in the back of my mind I am aware of a meaningless war going on. If I sound drained for a twenty-five year old, I am.

Mom seems a little better but far from her old self, if you know what I mean. Oh, I forgot to tell you, I'm here for the theater. Me and Liz and a bunch of us started one. It's no big deal but it's all I'm interested in right now. Are you married or even in love? Hope you are well.

Please write soon.

Love, Spud

FAMILY *(reading from a letter)*

December 8, 1966,

Dear Spud,

I was both pleased and disturbed to get your letter. I was pleased to hear from you, but disturbed to see you make a mistake in self-judgment. You are definitely NOT a flop. Neither Dad nor I nor anyone else in the family thinks so. I see real promise for your life and I have faith that you will continue to grow in your ability to understand life and to feel sympathetically and empathetically for people. However, you do devote much time in your letter to pot. I still think that the dangers inherent in induced visions are great. You speak of seeing a world in a devil's-food can top. I'm not sure I want to see it there.

I spent a total of just about a week at home over Christmas. I had to tell Dad (who really knows this underneath) that I did not find Mom substantially improved, in fact about the

same. I took the step of getting in touch with a good psychiatrist I know about in Cambridge.
With love,
Rocky
P.S. Mom and Dad were very happy with your wind chime.

ADVENTURE

I began to make harsh judgments not only against that theater, but against theater itself. I began to see it as a temporal art that had little power to effect social change. The Alley Theatre in Houston was there to please its audience, not to challenge them. I began to see it as little different than TV.

After all, who wants to play to an audience that calls up and says, "I want two front-row seats and make sure they're not next to no NEGRAS."

I could no longer contain my aggression toward that place. It had to raise its ugly head in some way and, at last, it did. As my stay at the Alley continued, I began to try to purify myself by going on a total soybean diet. Soybeans were plentiful there and I had just recently read of their protein value.

So, I began to eat soybeans morning, noon and night. It was during this soybean regimen that I was cast as the lead angel in the *World of Shalom Aleichem*.

It wasn't a very big role but I did get to wear a beautiful white, floor-length angel's robe. It made me feel like the

Immaculate Conception and I did get to lead all the other angels onstage.

It wasn't many evenings into the run before I realized that my soybean diet was causing enormous gas. It was that slow, hot kind with the proper muscle control you could ease out, burning your cheeks as it went, and then let it slowly drift as an inerasable cloud.

The gas would build up inside my angel's robe because it was floor length and lead weighted to make sure it stayed on the floor. So, it was a kind of natural gas tent and to make things worse, or better, I gave up wearing underwear under that robe.

So, there was a whole world going on there. A little gas works, and just to get that soup cooking more and mix up the colors more, I took to breaking my diet.

After the evening bowl of soybean, I'd have a dessert of apples and figs. This I discovered really did the trick. You see I hadn't learned to express my anger through the right orifice yet. I could feel it build up all hot and steamy, and on my cue, I would enter with all the other angels following. And trailing out from under my robe, a great wake of gas bubbles rose, while all the other angels wept behind me. I, on the other hand, kept the straight poker face of a good actor.

LOVE

I lost my virginity to Pam, and it was so traumatic that I swore off all sex for a year except for elaborate masturbation. I had met Pam at a party and picked her up there. We never went home together. We just did it in an empty bedroom at the apartment where the party was.

It was all so strange. I remember finding a warm wet place between her legs and trying to fill it up.

I was licking her breasts, not because I really wanted to but because for some reason I thought I should do it. And out of the clear blue she said, "What do you think I am, your mother?" and that's when I came, just like that. I hadn't been in her two minutes and I just shot off and it didn't feel any different than a sneeze, from my crotch instead of my nose.

After it was all over I had no idea what I had lost or what I had gained. I just wanted to get out of there, and I did.

JOURNALS
Journal entry 1967: I had a bottle of tequila and was sipping it outside the Providence Airport. Dad pulled up in his air-conditioned LTD and gave me one of his wiry greetings, a kind of uptight embrace without really touching. Our bodies on the verge of coming together. Me getting the vague impression that of his body as being held together by bailing wire.

He noticed the bottle or smelled the booze on my breath and said, "What, have you been tying one on?" He put my bags in the trunk and we got in the car together.

The air conditioning was a relief. We rode for a few miles in a sort of uncomfortable silence and I popped the question, "How's Mom?" "She's gone." Was all he said and he began to cry a horrid, wheezy, sad dried-up, crackle of a cry. I just sat there frozen like a statue. I didn't reach out to him.

I suddenly saw that dry August landscape go flat. The other cars passed with all their windows closed and all I could think was she's gone, she's gone; dies of a broken heart like in fairy tales. Like there and then suddenly not there. Trying to make sense of gone, I had an image of a dandelion when it turned to fluff *(blows)* gone. Died of a broken heart. We rode in silence. Dad weeping over the sound of the air-conditioner. The broken, hopeless landscape passed and went flat suddenly without color.

The next day Dad went to work. It amazed me that he was able to go to work but I supposed that helped him keep it all together. I stayed in the house all day and just felt the presence of my mother's absence. I went into Mom's walk-in closet. I looked at myself in her full-length mirror and then I looked at her shoes, a long row of empty shoes. How sad I felt and I thought of all that dental work she had done just before she killed herself.

Journal entry 1969: I know that I'm still all right because I still love, and have the sky, the seasons, the ocean. If things get any worse I can go to them and they will take me in. I often feel lost in the essence of a day, the mild wind and easy clouds, the graceful easy white ass of day, that I want nothing more than to become a leaf, not to write about it, but to do nothing, to be taken in and bathed. For me a perfect moment is when I'm being there and nowhere else in my mind.

FAMILY

At the end of my first trip to the West Coast I wound up, for some reason, in the Las Vegas jail. Cops had stopped me on my way home to my vibrating bed. When they'd asked for my name I had said, "Why do you ask?" After that things went real fast.

So I found myself that night having dinner in the prison cafeteria. One of the convicts named Vinnie said, "Anyone want my fucking carrots?" in a tone that sounded more like "What asshole here likes carrots?" I jumped at the offer and said, "Oh sure, yeah, I love carrots," and at that moment I realized I was too enthusiastic. I was a carrot lover, and I had shown my weakness and my vulnerability.

When Vinnie passed me his plate, the idea crossed my mind that nothing comes without consequences in any place, particularly that place.

Later that night, smoke, soot and embers were floating up around my bunk, and I thought, My God, the whole place is on fire. I sat up in a panic and looked over the edge of my bunk, and there were Vinnie and his friend Frank making a little campfire under the empty bunk below me. They were trying to toast some bread they had stolen from dinner. They had rolled up the mattress so that the metal surface of the bottom bunk was exposed, and then they had lit a whole roll of toilet paper under the bunk to heat it up.

The spongy white bread was lying like some strange artwork entitled "Wonder Bread on Gray Metal."

I went to sleep that night thinking I had to make a real effort to get the hell out of there. Finally after seven days, my girlfriend back in New York managed to get money to a bondsman, and I was released. I got out of Vegas as fast as I could and headed straight for the Grand Canyon.

I got there at sundown, perfect timing at last. The next morning I made my slow way down, deep into the bowels of Mother Earth. The hot, dry sun baked my newly freed body. I came upon a stream. It was crystal clear, a rushing transparency.

I pulled off my shorts and slipped into the stream. Its shocking coldness made all parts of me come together and immediately be there. Then some part of me surprised another part by yelling out, "Oh my good Christ! Oh shit! Oh God, it's cold!"

As I relaxed, I became all body wrapped in a transparent cocoon of rushing water. I lay there looking up at the massive rock walls. Here, I thought, I could lay to rest a part of me, let my raging past soar up and out of me. Above me, I saw all these ghosts. I saw Mom in her sundress and saddle shoes, stomping. I saw Dad spreading her ashes over the bay. I saw Vinnie and Frank, the two toast-cooking jailbirds, come out together from under my bunk bed, squinting and smiling in the sun. They all joined hands and danced a great boogie-woogie chain dance to heaven.

Exhausted by the hike and washed clean by the stream, I was emptied of past and future. For the first time in my life I realized something did matter, something mattered to me.

It was the sharing of all this, of the true story of some of the things that happened to me while living on this earth. I wanted to go to New York City and at last take the money Mom had left me to live on while I wrote it all down.

JOURNALS
Journal entry 1978: The unobserved life doesn't feel like living. Once I no longer felt God watching, I began to watch myself.

I have found that I like the fact that I have been writing everyday. I have been writing as though I was against a deadline and as I write now, I feel that good writing could help you to write your way out of almost anything.

I think of myself as a collagist taking bits and scraps from the growing heap of my life in order to create a more conscious narrative form. I came to know of my life through the telling of it.

ADVENTURE
I find myself down in the Bowery, which is a perfect place for me to be right now. I'm wandering through this gaggle of prostitutes who are working out of the john's cars. I'm walking past them, and I'm noticing out of the corner of my eye that there's this black Pontiac pulling up, and they're all rushing to it like flies.

They're over there all bunched around the Pontiac and I'm walking by, and one of them turns and yells, "Yo, hey, They want you!"

I turn, because I'm curious, and I love to be wanted.

I move closer, and the prostitutes part, like the Red Sea. I walk right through, and see this old black Pontiac with three Hasidic Jews in it, two in the front and one in the back.

And they say, "Get in."

And I do... I figured I was safe. I didn't think anyone could impersonate a Hasidic Jew. I mean, if there were three priests in the car, I would not have gotten in.

I sat in the back seat with the youngest one, and there was no sexual vibe in the car at all. I didn't know what they wanted, but there was no sexual vibe. We drive off, and the prostitutes are yelling, "Goodbye! have a good trick, babe! Have a good trick!"

We're riding in the car and my new companions say, "Do you want any beer or pizza?"

I say, "No, I never drink before five, and I've already eaten. So what's up?" By now I'm saying I'm a drifter from Schenectady. I've taken on this new identity. I wanted a vacation from Spalding Gray.

I say, "Where are we going?"

And they say, "We're taking you to Williamsburg to clean our synagogue."

I think, oh my God, well, why not? You know, it's a nice vacation; it's a nice way to tour New York. I've never been to Williamsburg; I don't believe we're going to do this.

But we did it. We drove over the Williamsburg Bridge, then pulled up in front of this small synagogue. I go in and all these Hasidim are there, with twinkling eyes, looking up at me like little Santa Clauses. They're repairing the bindings on old books. They take me to the back door, and, listen, I know that at any point I can just walk out. But I'm not doing that. I'm taking it in. They give me a dustpan and a rake and a broom and a shovel, and they say, "Clean. Please, clean our backyard."

I go into the backyard and I start raking. I'm feeling great.

I'm raking up the leaves, I am sweeping up the broken white plastic knives and forks left over from parties, and I'm whipping it up! I'm doing such a great, energized job that this woman who lives in the building behind the synagogue throws open her windows and cries out, "Hey! You work good! You come here next?"

I say, "I'm all booked up. Sorry. This is it for the day."

In an hour's time I have that whole backyard just perfect. The Hasid who was driving the car comes down and says, "You work good. You are the best, hardest-working Bowery bum we have ever picked up." It turns out that every

Sunday they go and pick up Bowery bums and bring them over to clean the place.

He says. "Usually we just give them drinks, but you don't drink, so we have to pay you. How much, huh? Eight. I think eight dollars."

I say, "No, no, ten… It's ten dollars an hour."

"Eight plus carfare." he says.

"No, ten and I'll walk." I answer.

"No. Eight."

Here we are, a Scot and a Jew, haggling over money in the back of a synagogue. I get the ten dollars and I walk. I'm walking over the Brooklyn Bridge back to the city feeling triumphant!

LOVE

You know who I dated most when I was in boarding school and college? My mother. We'd go to see Bergman films and discuss them afterwards. Go see *Ben Hur* because she was very religious. Go see *Tom Jones* and she'd get very upset because, "How could a scoundrel get away with that?" We'd have discussions like that so there was no room, or I didn't allow it, or there was some sort of guilt in there, but there was no room for a lot of dates.

I guess the first real date I went on was with Renee, and that was when I was thirty-seven or thirty-eight years old.

The *Soho News* was giving me an award for best performance in a play that my ex-girlfriend of twelve years had directed. The awards ceremony and the party afterwards were at Studio 54. I had never been to Studio 54 and I was really excited about having a look at it.

(JOURNALS lifts radio onto desk as disco music plays under next few lines.)

Studio 54. Everyone was dancing. I was dancing, and moving around the space and partying up and having a good time. And I looked across the crowded room (it was just like that) and I saw Renee's face. I had no idea who she was. But what struck me was the absolute openness in her face, the devilishness, the jollity. The "Hey you'd be a mensch if you could take me on." Usually if I'm going after a woman, I go after bodies. But what struck me about Renee was the fun in her face.

We had some drinks. And then I don't know if we made the agreement there, that we were going back to her place, or whether I just walked her back and she invited me up. It's all kind of amnesia to me how it led to us getting into bed. I mean, in those days it wasn't a big issue.

Anyway, somewhere right at the beginning of making love, she said, "Excuse me, but I think I'm going to throw up." I didn't take it personally. I politely got up and let her go down the hall to the bathroom.

She might remember it differently, but I think I went to see if she was all right and then we came back to bed and went to sleep. The throwing up, in fact, was delightful. It bonded us. It's like getting to know someone very quickly in a very intimate way.

JOURNALS

Journal entry 1982: Sometimes when I go to the Grand Union now, I usually go around three times a week, and those damn lines...when I get in the line, just to do something I get a *People* magazine and look in and see what happened to all of my now-famous friends. You know, see what's become of them.

I open it up. I went to school with Henry Winkler at Emerson College. And I say, "Oh, my God, look at this! Henry's making $90,000 each time he does a "Happy Days" show! Christ! I haven't even got health insurance and I'm thirty-nine years old!"

What else does it say? Wait a minute, Henry's had a child! He has a son! Wait a minute! Did I not have a son because I didn't have any money or was it a choice, or...now, wait a minute!

And then it comes. This little, dark voice. Like the devil.

Like...I don't know where it comes from and it says, "Henry's famous. He's got money. And what—maybe... also...he's HAPPY!"

(JOURNALS hits play on tape player on his desk. Theme from "The Tonight Show" plays as CAREER enters. On-stage-performers clap and make a fuss as if ushering a

guest onto "The Tonight Show" stage. CAREER takes place at a straight mike stand, lit with a classic cabaret-style circle of downlight—all very show biz—and gestures to cue the radio off. "Tonight Show" theme ends abruptly as radio is turned off and CAREER begins.)

CAREER

The next thing I was considered for was "The Tonight Show." The producers wanted to screen me first, so one of Johnny's representatives called me in for a rather intense two-hour interview. He got me rolling on stories and said, "Oh, very good, very good, but you're a little dark. Try to censor yourself a little more." The one he liked the best was about Adriana Glick, my first sensual girlfriend, at Emerson College. We used to make love in front of my fireplace in which I burned the leftover set from a college production of Molière's *The Misanthrope*.

When I finished the story, he said, "Oh, I like that very much, but listen, don't say the word "Misanthrope." Johnny hates theater.

"Basically you're playing to a bunch of not-overly intelligent people who want to go to sleep. You get too high-falutin'. You go light and then you get heavy, you're not a good self-editor. But I love your stories. Do you have any more? Do you have any therapist stories?"

"Oh, yeah, I have one about my first therapist. I was always trying to make him laugh or make him talk or just get him to react to me in some way. He was a complete stone face, the kind of guy who if you didn't speak to him, he wouldn't speak back and you could sit for the entire session in silence. But one day I happened to be telling him a story about my father, who is a creature of habit.

"He has little bedtime rituals. He's not a very metaphysical man, nor is he in any way superstitious. But he always puts his slippers right by the bed.

"One night my brother Rocky was hiding under the bed (Rocky must have been about fourteen), and after my father parked his slippers, Rocky just reached out, grabbed the slippers and threw them straight up in the air.

"My father yelled to my mother, 'Betty, come quick! My slippers are flying! My slippers are flying!' And my therapist laughed."

Johnny's rep said "Oh, that's good, that's good, love it, have you got any more?"

I said, "I do, about my second therapist…oh, wait, wait a minute, no. That one starts funny but ends with Auschwitz."

"No, thank you. Listen, Spalding, really, I love you, I love you really. I think you'd go over well on "The Dick Cavett Show."

I said "Yeah? Well, I'd love to be on it."

"It hasn't been on for years."

I said, "Oh, really? I didn't know that."

He said, "You didn't know "The Dick Cavett Show" was off the air? I love it! I love it, but I don't believe you. Listen, you've got to realize that being on the Johnny Carson show is not a whole lot of fun.

You can't just chitchat. You'll be on the spot. You gotta go for the jugular. Johnny's going to be interviewing you. He has to know all the questions before you go on. He's got to be in control. For starters, you should prepare four questions for him. Okay? You've got a TV, right?

"Yeah, we've got one."

"Well, would you watch the show for the next week? And get a feel how you might fit in? Would you promise me that? And then, let's talk again at the end of the week and see if you can come up with those four questions."

So, I gave it a try, but unfortunately I fell asleep almost every night before Johnny came on. It wasn't that I didn't want to get on the show, I had nothing against it.

I would love to capture the American imagination. Who wouldn't? It's just that everyone goes to bed early in L.A.

Johnny's producer called and said, "Have you thought of four questions?"

And I said, "I really haven't given it much thought. But I did come up with a good opener."

"What is it?"

"Well, the first question might be, 'Why is this night different from any other night?'" He didn't laugh, he was Italian.

JOURNALS

Journal entry 1988: Q. Let's return to religion. Your mother was a Christian Scientist. What were the positive aspects of Christian Science?

FAMILY

   1 - silent prayer
   2 - being able to stay home from school
   3 - early exposure to insanity

JOURNALS. What was positive about early exposure to insanity?

FAMILY. Well it gave me a kind of a road into what I now refer to as the poetics of anxiety. A feeling, a very real feeling that we live in apocalyptic times and much of my work has been about that end-of-the-world philosophy of emotions that Christian Science chronicles.

But now I'm taking the positive step toward writing.

JOURNALS. What do you hope for?

FAMILY. Health insurance. I think I could do without the swimming pool if I could only swing health insurance.

JOURNALS. One last question. Why are you interviewing yourself?

FAMILY. I couldn't wait. I'm very impatient. It's the child in me. You know, because I'm not an actual father. I'm still the father of the child that is in me.

ADVENTURE

The first message to come off the machine is from HBO. They want me to do a new HBO special in which I travel around the United States interviewing people who have just been taken aboard flying saucers. And I call them back and say, "Oh yeah! No, no, it's not an insult at all. You've' come to the right person. It's right up my alley. No, no, I'm sure they're out there... No but I'll tell you what... No, I can't talk now but I'll be down soon to talk about the details."

The next message is from an independent filmmaker from India. He's had an epiphany. He's seen the poster for *Swimming to Cambodia* and he's had an epiphany that he must bring me down to the Kumbamaila, which is a religious festival that happens every seven years where three holy rivers come together in a great maelstrom. And two million people gather on the edge of it and start hurling themselves in. And he wants to take me there, throw me in, and film my reaction. This is the only call that Renee intercedes on. I hear her from the other room yelling, "Spald, do not return that call!"

CAREER

Which is how I found myself at CAA. If you don't know what CAA is, it is the largest talent agency in the universe, I would say. It's the mafia of talent agencies. It controls the

American economy. I walked in and sat down at their big table. There's this round table, a marble table, and they were all there. About ten of them—men and women all suntanned, windblown, and healthy. Oh so healthy! There's no more drugs in Hollywood. Health is the new drug. Those people have been up since five in the morning doing kung fu, jogging, reading scripts and eating blue-green algae from the bottom of the Oregon lakes. I'm telling you I walked in there and they were ready! I have never walked into a room and felt such a sense of readiness in my life. There was nothing happening, but they were ready for it in case it did. I walked in, and the man at the head of the table offered me the only drug left in Hollywood—a can of Diet Coke.

Then he leaned in and said, "Uh, thank you very much for taking time from your busy schedule to come to meet with us. We'd all like to begin by telling you that we all hope you're not one of those artists that's afraid to make money."

And I said, "Um, how much money are we talking about?"

"Well, we did the seventeen-million-dollar Stallone deal."

"S-s-seventeen? Uh, s-s-seventeen million d-dollars, right? A-all for Sylvester?"

"That's right."

I was conflicted. I didn't know whether to say "Congratulations" or "You should be shot at sunrise." I just hoped that Sylvester had good charities he was giving to.

And I said, "What I'm really curious about is how did you guys find out about me?"

And he said, "We saw your film, *Swimming to Cambodia*, and I never thought I could watch anyone talk for eighty-seven minutes, particularly another man."

"What movie theater did you see it in?"

"We saw it here in the office on tape."

"But it's not out on video yet."

"We have our ways."

"Well could you do me a favor because my father, um, my father didn't get to see it because it showed in an art cinema in Providence, Rhode Island, and they didn't have any matinees, and he wouldn't miss cocktail hour."

Then he just reaches around and pulls what looks like a piece of plastic tubing right out from the wall, and speaking into it in a low, devilish voice, says, "Get Spalding Gray's father a copy of *Swimming to Cambodia*, will you please?"

But I didn't sign.

LOVE

I'm working on my book, my novel, and I'm almost finished. Brewster North—as I'm calling myself— has made it to Australia.

But it's driving him nuts because he is surrounded on the beach by all these beautiful bare-breasted Australian women. And he can't get near them. He's trying to be loyal to his girlfriend. He's getting so turned on by these women that he can't bear it. He's trying to push his libido down and you can't keep that stuff down.

He gets back to the hotel and he's trying to relieve himself with these ornate masturbation rituals. He's right-handed and he's working a lot with his left hand to try to surprise himself, and he's having a wild time with a Hoover vacuum cleaner. But the sound of it is so distracting that he's wrapped it in a blanket, and put it in the closet and has run the hose out under the door.

I've just taken that section to my typist, a spinster from Queens. Every time I go in to see her, I'm always looking over to see what she thinks of the book, because she's the only one who's read it. But she never gives an inch. She acts totally professional. This time I come in and pick up this new section of writing, look it over, try to catch her eye. But she doesn't look back. She gets up and moves like a great tortoise across her kitchen, lights a Virginia Slim, then looks over at me and says, "Well, Mr Gray, you're definitely a writer. But I hope this is fiction or you're in real trouble."

JOURNALS

Journal entry 1990: Whenever I start work on a new monologue I think of this exercise we used to do back in the old
experimental theater days. A bunch of us would couple up
in different parts of the room and, sitting on the floor with
our legs spread, we'd grasp each other's forearms and rock
back and forth until we're exhausted and then fall into each
other's arms and whisper a secret to them we had never
told before. My only problem was I didn't have any secrets
I'd never told before, not one.

FAMILY

When I was in therapy about two years ago, one day I noticed that I hadn't had any children. And I like children at a
distance. I wondered if I'd like them up close. I wondered
why I didn't have any.

I guess I had always fantasized that if and when I had a
child it would be in Northern California. We, me and some
sweet hippie beauty I was living with, would have a water
birth or the child would be brought into the world by a
midwife in a teepee somewhere. I always thought that one
day it would all, at last, happen to me in Northern California. In fact, I had begun to define my life as what I did
while waiting to move to Northern California.

ADVENTURE

I went out and it was winter in Minneapolis. A group of
us—I think there were probably seventeen of us, men and
women—did this incredible ceremony that Azaria Thornbird led with a peace pipe, where she called all the Indian

spirits from the four directions. We were all inside a tent, sitting naked in a circle on straw which is laid over the snow. It's dark and it's cold in there because no hot rocks have been brought in yet.

Azaria instructs us that the sweat ceremony could last quite a long time, two or three hours. Toward the end of the prayers, we'd pray to give away some thing, some condition that we no longer wanted.

But, she warns us, in no case—in no case—should we identify with what another person gives away. Because if we take it on, we're going to be in trouble. So just pass it on; don't identify with it, just pass it on, and let it go out of the tent.

After that she will come and pour cold water over the rocks, and we're supposed to sit in silence and listen to the hot rocks steam—and they often actually speak and give us valuable information. That's what Azaria told us.

I like this very much, this whole very ritualized ceremony.

I like it. I just hope that people don't go on. I mean there are seventeen people in there, after all, and I hope the prayers aren't too long, because it's going to get real hot.

People begin praying.

"O Great Spirit, this is Robert speaking and I want to remain humble and get rid of my macho qualities for this ceremony. I have spoken."

It comes around to me, and I say, "O Great Spirit, this is Spalding speaking, and I pray that I can maintain a sincere and open attitude in this ceremony and not pollute it with my heady analysis and ironic commentary and end up turning this sacred event into just another story that I will try to sell to the American public."

And the entire tent goes, "Ho! Ho! Ho! Ho! Ho!" Which is a kind of supportive cheer to say, let's see if you can pull that one off.

More hot rocks are brought in. Now it's starting to get a little hot. Oh man, I know what they mean by sweat! And my God, I've got my nose down on the ground trying to breathe fresh air from under the bottom of the tent.

And all I can see is the sign on the outside of the steam bath at my health club in New York City that says DO NOT EXCEED FIFTEEN MINUTES UNDER ANY CIRCUMSTANCES! And I'm thinking, Who is this Azaria Thornbird, anyway?! How long have I been in here? What's going on?

More hot rocks are brought in, lots. Now the place is really hot; the place is reeking. People are down on their sides, choking; they can't breathe. My pulse is up to 160. Another round of prayer starts; we're supposed to give something away. I can't wait to pray. I'm telling you I feel like my heart is going to explode. I've got my hand on my pulse, it's so hot I can't breathe, and people are praying.

"O Great Spirit, this is Susan speaking. I want to give away my gluttony. I have spoken."

It comes round to me and I say, "O Great Spirit, this is Spalding speaking. And I want to give away the fear that I'm about to have a heart attack at this very moment!"

And just as I say this the guy next to me, who is about my age, leaps up and runs out of the tent screaming, "My heart is popping! My heart is popping! My heart is popping!"

And I'm FINE!

My pulse slows down. He's just taken all my fear and run right out the door with it.

Azaria says, "Someone has broken the sacred circle here. The power has gone out of the sweat.

Now listen, we're going to do the fourth round of prayers where we'll listen to the rocks talk. If any of you feels you have to go, you must leave now. Because when this flap shuts, you're in."

Oh my. Now I at the same time am very claustrophobic and find it difficult to take orders. But I am determined to ride this thing out. I sit hard and I just hope that the hot rocks don't talk too long, you know?

She says, "I'm closing the flaps." She closes it, and this guy who's a member of the lodge, with a ponytail down to his ass, leaps up and charges for the flap. She throws her naked body in front of him and says, "Get back Lame Deer! GET BACK!"

He hurls himself back on the hay crying, "Shit, fuck, fuck, fuck." Everyone's holding him down, chanting, "Ho! Ho! Ho! Ho! Ho!" Everyone's Ho-ing him, Ho-ing him, Ho-ing him until at last he's calm.

We sit there panting, and we listen to the hot rocks talk. I didn't understand a word.

CAREER

I answer the phone and it's Gregory Mosher, the director of Lincoln Center Theater, saying, "Listen, Spalding, how would you like to play the Stage Manager in Thornton Wilder's *Our Town* on Broadway?"

I can't believe what I'm hearing and I say, "Gregory, listen, thank you very much. I am honored, but I don't think I could do it. I simply don't think I could say those lines. They're too wholesome and folksy. Get Garrison Keillor."

"We don't want Garrison Keillor, we want you. We want your dark, New England, ironic sensibility."

"Well, Gregory, you got me there. I'll tell you what. Give me a day to think about it."

I hang up. I think, My God! This is a chance of a lifetime. Here it is. It's a limited run. The role is great. I could speak from my heart at last—provided I could memorize the lines—and I could at last use my New England accent.

So I think I'd better just call my Hollywood agent, see if she has any opinions on this before I say yes or no.

I call her up and she says, "Dear heart, dear heart! No way! Why, after all these years of acting, would you want to be a stage manager?"

So I say yes.

Much to my surprise, I find that I love doing the play because I'm able to get in touch with Thornton Wilder's language. I get swept back to New England where I came from. I get swept back to New England where I used to believe in God and eternity and all the things the play is about.

The cemetery scene is the most powerful for me. You see, Emily dies in childbirth and her funeral takes place on stage in the third act. And when the mourners exit, Emily dressed in a simple white dress walks across the stage to sit in the straight-backed chair that represents her grave.

And she sits down amongst all the other recent dead who are all sitting bolt upright, staring up at the stars above. Everyone is so peacefully concentrated. Franny Conroy, who is playing Mother Gibbs, is sitting in the front row. She has been doing transcendental meditation for the past fifteen years and she's in a deep trance.

The little boy playing Emily's brother, Wally Webb, is an eleven-year-old boy, and he is sitting there, as well, not blinking for forty minutes while I talk about eternity. And in the play I say, "And they stay here while the earth part of them burns away, burns out... They're waitin' for something they feel is comin'. Something important, and great. Aren't they waitin' for the eternal part in them to come out clear?"

And every night I would perform this and every night it would basically be the same.

Except often, when you do a long run of a play you have what I call a unifying accident, in which something so strange happens in the play, that it suddenly unites the audience in the realization that we are all here together at this one moment in time. It's not television. It's not the movies. It happened as I was speaking of the dead and I say, "And they stay here while the earth part of them burns away, burns out... They're waitin' for something they feel is comin'. Something important and great..." As I say this, I turn and gesture to them, waiting, and, just as I turn and gesture, the little eleven-year-old boy playing Wally Webb projectile vomits! Like a hydrant it comes, hitting some of the dead on their shoulders! The other dead levitate out of their chairs, in total shock, around him and drop back down. Franny Conroy, deep in her meditative trance, is slowly wondering, "Why is it raining on stage?" The little boy flees from his chair, vomit pouring from his mouth. Splatter. Splatter. Splatter. I'm standing there. My knees are shaking. The chair is empty. The audience is thunderstruck!

There is not a sound coming from them, except for one little ten-year-old boy in the 8th row. He *knows* what he saw... He is laughing!

At this point, I don't know whether to be loyal to Thornton Wilder and go on with the next line as written, or attempt what might be one of the most creative improvs in the history of American Theater. At last I decide to be loyal to Wilder and simply go on with the next line, and I turn to the empty chair and say, "Aren't they waitin' for the eternal part in them to come out clear?"

JOURNALS

Journal entry 1992: I went to a Chinese deli to buy water and when I walked out I had a very blissful moment, could almost call it a perfect moment. I watched a fast-blowing cloud break up and go through the most extreme colors of turquoise to magenta. I felt suddenly free and open and not in need.

For me, the bubbles are often perfect moments that lift me out of my sadness and despair.

I can't be creative without being self-destructive because I'm like Humpty Dumpty. There are two me's deeply built in. The smasher and the rebuilder. I am both Humpty and the king's men. I am both lost and found.

FAMILY

I'd come back to do a theater workshop on Block Island. My father lived near the train station in Kingston, Rhode Island, and I asked him to pick me up and drive me to the Block Island ferry. I thought we could have a good visit in the car.

At the train station Dad gave me that old obligatory bundle-of-wire hug and we rode in silence. Close to the ferry, he said, "You know Rock—Chan—Spud"—whenever he forgot which son he was with, he called all three names out—"I was thinking, if we miss the ferry, we could have a beer together."

"What do you mean, Dad?"

He said, "We could go to my summer cottage, if we miss the ferry."

I said, "Well, let's miss it."

"What do you mean?" He said.

"I can get another one in an hour!" I answered.

Every summer my stepmother and father would rent a cottage by the sea and never use it. They'd just leave it locked up; it was like an idea. And he wanted to go to it. So I said, "Let's go," and he did a U-turn in the car—I'd never seen him do that—and off we went. He opened the cottage for the first time that summer and it was all mildewed in there, and he got out the cocktail munchies.

They were all fog-bound: wilted Cheez Doodles, soggy pretzels, those lite peanuts that are like Styrofoam and two teeny cans of Budweiser—not my favorite beer, not my favorite-size can. But it was a drink with Dad!

We went to the picnic table out back near the water's edge and oh, God, this heavy Rhode Island fog was coming in; thick pea-soup fog. It was like the opening of a Eugene O'Neill play.

We sat there in silence until I broke it and said, "Well, Dad, I guess it's good we have this chance to talk. I don't think we've talked since I was fourteen and you told me the facts of life on a golf course. But I was wondering, now that you're about to be eighty, do you have any regrets? Because I sometimes feel that my life is ruled by regret. I have so many. Do you have any, Dad?"

"Nope. Just that I never climbed Mount Katahdin." *(Either FAMILY or another cast member makes the sound of a foghorn.)*

(Gestures to sound and explains.) Sound of foghorn.

"You know, Gram Gray once told me that you and Mom were married in the white church in Barrington on Halloween. "What a kinky, imaginative day to get married on. Why'd you do that, Dad?"

"Seemed as good a day as any." *(FAMILY or other cast repeats foghorn sound.)*

"You know, you had three children, you had three boys. I never had any children, I don't know why—I don't know if it's by mistake or that I'm afraid to have them, or if I can't have them.

What did you get out of having them, why would anyone have children?"

"That was the thing to do in those days." *(FAMILY or other cast member repeats foghorn sound.)*

"Well, I won't bother you anymore. But I did want to ask you one more question. You had three boys, I was the middle son. Dad, why was I the only one that wasn't circumcised?"

Long pause.

"You weren't?"

Then I said, "Well, I guess we better get going."

And Dad said, "Oh all right, pack it up. Yep, yep. Lock up, lock up."

We locked up the house. We got outside and he realized he hadn't called my stepmother, Sis, to find out what kind of fish to bring home from the Galilee market, and he said, "Oh shit! I forgot to call Sis."

Then he unlocked the door and went back in to call, and I thought, My father never said "shit" in front of me in his life. He came back out and I realized I'd left my Danish school bag in there.

The cottage was locked up again and I said, "Oh shit, Dad, I left my Danish school bag in there." And then I realized we had just bonded. Those two "shits" made all the difference. I told this story at my father's memorial service. I did. My stepmother said afterward, "You're crazy. You're on drugs. Your father never said that word in his life. Don't you ever come back to Rhode Island as long as you live!"

CAREER

I'd entered what Renee's mother calls the Bermuda Triangle of Health. She says that between fifty and fifty-three years old is the Bermuda Triangle of Health. Things start going wrong with you then. I was coming into it—with a macula pucker in my left eye. I was called in by my eye doctor for an examination, because he wanted to see if my condition was deteriorating. I go back to that waiting room. They dilate my pupils; I'm sitting there in the waiting room, waiting in the fuzz.

I see this person come out of my doctor's office. In my dilated condition I see this little guy backing out in a pinstripe suit, making real jerky movements, kind of like in a Buster Keaton movie. He's waving like a wind-up toy. Like he's this...automatic something, I don't know what.

He turns and starts walking toward me. I'm amazed and shocked to see that he's got on one of those rubber Nixon masks that we used to buy in joke shops when Nixon was president. What the hell is going on in my doctor's office? He's walking right toward me, and as he gets closer I realize that it is Richard Nixon.

Richard Nixon is walking directly toward me—with intent. As though he were going to come up to me and say, "Hi, I saw *Swimming to Cambodia*, and I loved it!"

I think, No, wait a minute, maybe his pupils are dilated too, and he thinks I'm Ralph Lauren.

He walks right up to me, and I say, "Oh hi."

He says nothing, and then he walks out. He just leaves. I go into my doctor's office and I say, "Was that Richard Nixon who just left here?"

"Oh yes, nothin' the matter with him."

"Well, there is no justice in the world, is there."

LOVE

I go out for a walk in New York City to try to be fully alive. I walk to Washington Square Park, basically a dysfunctional fountain with broken benches around it.

And I walk around that fountain obsessing on what I could do to feel more fully alive. Well, okay, so I'm obsessing about Kathie, a woman I had met on the road who had moved to New York and had sent me her phone number. Should I call her, should I "touch base" with her? Drop in for some tea?

I was attracted to Kathie partly because she was a mother, she had her hands full raising her six-year-old daughter. This was important for me because she had no leftover mothering energy to direct toward me. If I get a whiff of that mothering energy I just *suck it dry!*

Also I'm dwelling on the fact that I'm going to turn fifty-two years old, and I'm thinking about my mom, and how she committed suicide at fifty-two, and did that mean I was gonna do it too? And around that dysfunctional fountain I go, peeling the onion of my mind, running into the same Jamaican drug dealers each time around, not recognizing I'm the same person, trying to sell me the same drugs each time, saying "Hey man, what's happening?"

"Hey, good question, what IS happening?" I reply.

Now, things really started to heat up the closer I got to the big crisis year of fifty-two. I started muttering to myself and involuntarily shouting out, but no one really noticed that in New York City. Mom let out with a few of these yelps in a Rhode Island supermarket and they put her in a straitjacket. If Mom had lived in New York, she might be alive today.

To complicate things even more, it was around that time that my longtime girlfriend Renee re-expressed her desire to get married, and I felt that I should be able to give that to her as a gift. I also thought that once I married her, it would put an end to the affair with Kathie. But at the same time I was so nervous about it all, I had to propose in front of my therapist, who knew I was having an affair and said nothing about that.

When I got married it was like a cork in a glass bottle, and I started feeling, Oh, help, I can't breathe, let me out.

The affair with Kathie heated up. Oh, I thought it was just going to STOP. I thought just by my getting married it would peter out. And when Kathie told me she was pregnant, I fell down on the floor and went into a fetal position.

Out of all that hazy hell of disintegration, I can remember one moment clearly. My wife Renee called me to talk about something and we were interrupted by the call waiting, which I took; I hear this raspy voice say, "Good morning. This is Kathie's mom and I just want to tell you that you are the father of a beautiful baby boy."

JOURNALS

Journal entry 1995: I have to tell you that the freedom of choice is almost unbearable for me. I often find myself thinking more about the road not taken than the one I took. As a result, I am a very messy chooser. I tend to get paralyzed by the choice, then freak out, short circuit, act out and drive everyone nuts. I'm a passive person and I don't want to be ashamed of that passivity. I want to make it work.

FAMILY

I wanted to see my son; after all, I'd never seen him and now he was eight months old. I was completely unaware that this was a long time. I was under the impression that once a baby, always a baby.

I guess I thought of six years old as the end of babyhood. I had no idea that eight months was quite a way along in the development of a child.

I called Kathie and went to see them. She woke the baby, lifted him out of the crib, and he went right for her breast. When I saw that, I knew there was no need for a blood test. I saw the back of my father's head in his head. I saw my brother Rocky's eyes. I saw a distant mirror, I saw a little lust flower.

I saw a glorious accident. I saw a completely formed, whole human being, and I experienced a perfect paradox at that moment; I knew now that I could die and that I had to stay alive to help this little guy through.

Kathie had a radical plan. She said, "You haven't seen him for eight months, you should go bond with him. Take him off alone, to your summer house in the country."

And I did. I thought it was a completely mad idea, but I didn't question it. I was on the train to Brewster North with this eight-month-old creature, who was in my arms. I assumed he was beautiful, because everyone on the train kept stopping to say, "Oh my goodness, what a lovely grand-daughter you have." And when I got up to the house, I put him on the floor like a rug rat, a hamster, a cat or a dog— let him do his thing; while I do my thing—get out the bloody mary mix, the salmon, the green peas and prepare dinner. And then I had to change his diaper.

Bending over him, I looked down into his eyes and I fell in.

I did not expect the gaze that came back, it was absolutely forever. Long, pure, empty, not innocent, because way beyond innocence, mere being, pure consciousness, the observing self that I'd always been trying to catch was staring back at me; they were no-agenda eyes. Clear, open, not blinking, not judging, not tempting, not needing, not hurting, not consoling. Just pure—not old, not new, because not in time. And I just stared until I blinked. And had to pull away. I couldn't go on anymore in there.

I took him in my arms and we were together for five hours. He ate with me, in my lap. And when I chewed my green peas, he reached into my mouth and took them out to feed himself. I got the image of Mother Bird, Mother Robin, the way they spit the food into their babies' mouths. So I took his little head and, holding it, went to spit the green peas into his mouth like a mother bird, and he gave me a straight arm. And I thought, My God, he's got boundaries! Where would he get them at eight months? I could learn something from him. His dad doesn't have them at fifty-two!

LOVE

There's always been another woman, over my shoulder, over there, over there, but there's never just another son. You don't say "Hey look at that son." "Hey, look at the tush on that son."

No, there was a new kind of love going around in this new family. It was so different from the one-on-one, the only love I'd known before. This love alternated like a chain of broken-circuit Christmas lights. I loved Marissa for the way she loved her brother. I loved my son Forrest for the way he loved his mom, and turned her into a mother before I could, leaving me to know and love her for the woman she is.

CAREER

Friends and relatives were very supportive of our decision to have another child. The first slightly negative, not exactly supportive voice that we encountered came that summer on a beach in Martha's Vineyard. A man came up to us and said to me, "You look familiar," and I just said "I am." Now this guy on the beach did not exactly think my cute response was funny. He said, "No, I know, you're the guy that did that monologue at the Playhouse in Vineyard Haven where you talk about marrying your girlfriend while you're having an affair, and then you make the woman you're having the affair with pregnant.

"Then you seem to have a nervous breakdown as a result of all of this when it really should be your new wife that was breaking down."

"Please," I said. "No, more. I don't need a synopsis of what I already know too well and can't forget."

Then this guy on the beach looked over at Kathie, who was standing very pregnant at the water's edge while holding Forrest's hand, and he said, "Is that the woman you made pregnant?" I nodded yes and he said "and she's pregnant again?" to which I nodded again yes, and then he said, "Well, my goodness, you really are going for total immersion, aren't you?" Then he turned to me and asked "Do I look familiar to you?" to which I replied, "Not really."

He introduced himself as Peter Kramer, the author of *Listening to Prozac*. Meanwhile Kathie's sister who was at a distance, thought he was Martin Short and was waving all during our conversation and calling out, "I just loved you in *Father of the Bride*!"

ADVENTURE

What a strange, strict, quick imagination my stepdaughter Marissa has. I remember we had a dinner party and this woman was talking intensely about her deep belief in the possibility for human change. "We can all change if we really want to," she said, to which Marissa replied, "Yes, I believe in change. Look at the Unabomber, for example. He was a professor and he became a bomber."

JOURNALS

Journal entry 1997: I think I shut my heart down to protect myself from Mom's sadness. But the children opened my heart.

They have been a blessing and these memories burn in my heart like religious icons:

A: Marissa toasting me on my birthday for bringing her brother Forrest into the world.

B. Me and Forrest on the way to Martha's Vineyard in that old Ford Escort and when I was so hot and lost, outside Providence. Forrest who was sleeping in his car seat beside me woke and kissed me.

C: And most certain by Theo's face at birth and the honest confusion it expressed. I just looked down at him and saw this big WHY? expression coming back at me. He seemed to be asking me: Why this? Why something and not nothing?

ADVENTURE

I remember the first time I rode over the Sag Harbor bridge on my new bike just after moving here. I remember the feeling of what I can only call a complicated present. By that I mean where I am present and in the past at the same time.

It was because the place was so familiar in a very old sense and yet, at the same time, new. I felt as though I'd come home to Rhode Island without quite having to go there.

Standing there on that bridge for the first time, I felt as if I had returned to the place that I started from and was about to know it for the first time. Circles are, I think, so important to me, or to us. Circles are important because we only live once. Repeating, or coming around full circle, gives us the feeling of rebirth, of living again.

So, after thirty years of self-imposed exile from my land of islands and sea, I came full circle, and as I stood there on that bridge the idea occurs to me that if I wrapped my arms around myself, and just stood there so very, very still, I would feel that I had at last come home. I would feel connected to this place, this single place on Earth.

I stood there for the longest time, just waiting, but I never felt the stillness. All I felt was motion all around and under me. Like the water flowing under that very bridge. I had the realization that it is all transiency, impermanence, and change. So I felt the only appropriate thing to do was be in motion, so I got on my bike and rode.

(Loud abrasive sound rises at end of previous story and comes to a crash as it finishes, sort of an abstracted car crash. Piles of notebooks fall. The ground has shifted.)

LOVE

Our car spun around three times, that's how hard he hit, and drove the engine right into the front seat of the car, where Kathie burned her arm. Somehow she got out. I thought Kim, who was next to her, was dead. His forehead was down on the dashboard. Tara Newman was yelling, "The car's going to explode. Everyone get out!" I don't remember getting out, but the next thing I knew I was lying in the road next to Kathie.

It was a country hospital and they put me in a dormitory with five other men that are bashers and crashers; mainly, I think farmers, or guys that have hit each other with trucks and tractors, for fun or out of drunkenness, and they're all boasting about it on their cell phones, because cell phones have taken over Ireland, as they have America.

I was completely disheveled because I had no pajamas, no toothbrush. I guess you have to carry those with you, the Irish do that, in case of an accident.

The next morning is Sunday and the priest comes through with the Holy Eucharist and I take my First Communion, what can I tell you. I think, why not? Then a cross dresser comes through, I swear, it was out of a Fellini movie.

I will never forget her, him. He's got long green fingernails, balancing the toast between them and he's going, "Toast! Tea! Toast!"

Then a woman comes through and she's taking a survey: Do I want the hospital to be smoke free?

By noon the relatives of all the victims arrive with blenders and they start making daiquiris and margaritas. I wasn't offered any. They're watching the car races on television, going 192 miles per hour, and everyone is drinking. The TV is blaring, I'm alone, and oh, God, I feel a big caboose coming on. I've been constipated for two days. I call the nurse because I don't know what to do; I'm in traction, I can't get out of bed. They close the curtains and somehow, in a bedpan, they deliver this long brown snake.

It's the oddest angle I've ever taken a shit at. I don't know how they do it, not batting an eye. Who would do a job like that? It was like they were delivering a baby.

Then they opened the curtains and everyone just put down their forks and drinks and stared at me. I'm so excited that

I get my notebook out to write about it, and the other people are looking over at me as if to say, "Oh, another James Joyce have we here? Leave it to a Yank to take a shit in the middle of lunch and then write about it!"

(LOVE passes notebook to CAREER. Except for the journal entries, all of the accident stories will be read from the same notebook, the first time one story is happening to all the performers.)

CAREER
One of the nurses, when she found out I was actor, asked me

LOVE. "Are you in any scary movies? Because I like scary ones."

CAREER. I said, "No, not really."

LOVE. "No, not *The Exorcist*?"

CAREER: "No, just *The Killing Fields*, which is pretty scary."

LOVE. "Oh, no, I wouldn't know anything about killing fields. Any other movies then?"

CAREER. "Oh, *Beaches*."

LOVE. "Oh, yes, what did you play?"

CAREER. "The doctor."

LOVE. "Oh, sure enough, you were. Now, I remember it. What's Bette Midler really like?"

CAREER. "Oh, she's like herself, really. The only thing that I had problems with was when we had to do the kissing scene. She didn't want to kiss me, and I was hurt. I guess she thought I was a kiss-and-teller.

Finally, she did kiss me, and she said, "All right, now I've done it. Now, don't go telling the Wooster Group I kiss like Hitler."

(CAREER passes notebook to ADVENTURE.)

ADVENTURE

How to get out of this place? Kathie does everything she can to get me out of there. She somehow gets ahold of the head of the Irish Arts Council, Patrick Murphy, and he was able to get in touch with a hospital outside of Dublin, where they do special hip operations.

The morning of the operation—"We're taking you to the theater today, Mr. Gray." They're calling the operating room the theater. The anesthesiologist tries to talk me down by telling me about the glorious wars in the 1700s between Scotland and England, which I love, because he said that's how the Grays got over from Scotland to Ireland. It was unlike the anesthesiologist in New York Hospital who tried to talk me down by asking me if I had any contacts at NYU Film School for his son.

After the operation, which they told me was successful, so I shouldn't complain, they gave me this morphine drip for forty-eight hours, and that was a treat.

After the morphine, depression set in, and I didn't know whether to discuss it with the Irish. I didn't know if they recognized it. I mean, does a fish know it's swimming in water?

JOURNALS

Journal entry August 2001: When people say: but just think, you could be worse off, I also think but that's down the road. This accident does not cancel out all the other slings and arrows of outrageous fortune, no, no, no. But be positive, please, be positive!

Still, I keep thinking of the quote from Robert Lowell "The light at the end of the tunnel" is a train.

(FAMILY takes notebook from ADVENTURE.)

FAMILY

Back in the room we play scrabble. I'm not doing too well because I'm dyslexic and I can't even turn "war" into "wart."

Forrest is playing with his crash cars, and Theo is there, and Kathie looks up and sees this big dent in my forehead, where the bump was. She says, "My, God, you've got a huge dent in your forehead!"

I said, "Don't even say that!"

"It's so big I can stick my finger in it!"

"Oh, don't say that. Call a doctor!"

The doctor comes and says, "Sure enough. It's a dent then, oh, yes."

I said, "Why didn't you take an MRI? WE asked you to and you guys didn't take one. Why not, when I had a big bump there?"

"We're dealing with the hip. We didn't check on the head. We don't do that. We'll have to send you to another hospital." I say, "Well, I've got to get back to the states. I can't go to another hospital in Ireland."

We fly back to New York. I go to New York Hospital for an operation. I'm nervous about that. Andy Warhol died there under dubious circumstances.

The orderly that takes me down to the operation is from Dublin. The operation takes six hours. They cut me from ear to ear, peel down my forehead and put in a titanium plate. Bone splinters are released into my frontal lobe—I think they had to pick those out—from smashing my head against Kathie's head. They sew me up; it looks like I've had a facelift.

The fire alarm goes off at four a.m. and my nurse comes to tell me it's a false alarm. She just happens to be named Patricia Murphy. She's Irish. Her father was born in Tullamore, of all places, where the country hospital was that I was first in.

Is it a coincidence? I don't know. Is it fate?

Hmmm.

It gives me the creeps. I don't like it. My therapist believes in such things. I wonder if I should trust her?

(FAMILY steps away from mike, addressing audience. First time in play that there has been an unamplified voice. The lifesaving tools of the stage are beginning to break down.)

I've never been able to give advice before in my life. I've always been a relativist, and someone who felt that he didn't know.

Even as a father it's been difficult to say what exactly one should do and should not do in this world of confusing, relativistic, movable feast morality.

But I have to say that I now can give advice around one issue, or two issues: Always wear your seatbelt in the backseat of the car, which I'm sure you know, whether you do or not. And whatever you do, get an American Express Platinum card—its only $300 extra—so you can be medevacked the FUCK out of a foreign country if you get into an accident.

JOURNALS

Journal entry September 2002: It's as though I grew old in a flash. My timing is off. When I was in boarding school my drama instructor said I had good timing and that has held true throughout my career. That is until recently. For the past year, I've been cursed. I thought that writing this all down and doing the shows would help. It hasn't. Something just snapped.

Journal entry April 2003: I CAN NOT let the children see me go crazy. I can NOT play that one act on them. NO. Big NO because I am in the place of my mom now. The first thoughts of suicide came to me last month. After four months in Payne Whitney, I returned home where I kept riding out to that bridge on my bike just contemplating. Once I drove to the ocean and threw myself in. It was March and very cold. Someone at the beach saw me and called the police. The cop that stopped me knew a great deal of my work and said, "Oh yeah, you, your mother, and suicide. I've seen your stuff on TV. Because he's a fan he takes me home instead of back to the hospital. And I'm all wet.

Journal entry June 2003: Another hospital. This time UCLA Neuropsychiatric. Today is my birthday and they've just told me I have brain damage. The scar tissue is over my right frontal lobe and they don't know if it's from the accident or the surgery but they did say I was not a candidate for electric shock treatment—which I had twenty-one treatments of at NY Hospital. Titanium in my head and in my hip. I can't walk because of this drop foot, my forehead is disfigured and I feel like a guinea pig. They have me take all these stupid tests. The West Coast says brain damage and the East Coast says I'm depressed. They did tell Kathie that I will need twenty-four-hour care soon.

Journal entry September 2003: It was like out of a Bergman film when that guy at the block party asked me if I had any children or he asked which were mine and I lead him and his wife...I lead them on crutches. To show them out there at the end of the dock, framed by the rippling lake. The boys, Theo and Forrest, were sitting together and it was one of the most idyllic moments of my life. It was a proud perfect moment.

(Final journal entry to be read with eyes on page the whole time, not looking at audience.)

Journal entry December 2003: This is my last entry. Kathie, it's an old story you've heard over and over. My life is coming to an end. Everything's in my head now, my timing is all off. All this terrific hesitancy. In the last two years I've had at least ten therapists, maybe more, not to mention three psycho pharmacologists and all those shock treatments. Suicide is a viable alternative for me instead of going to an institution.

I don't want an audience. I don't want anyone to see me slip into the water.

(Lights dip to black and immediately begin a slow fade back up. Performers get up one by one, take notebooks from the floor, return to mikes and begin to read. In spite of the last action, the stories remain, the last moment does not negate the many other moments in the writing.)

FAMILY

That summer the bay was clear, with no algae. We could see all the way down to the bottom as we swam, and Mom and I would swim together. If I couldn't see everywhere, in all directions at once, which was of course was impossible, I'd go into a sort of panic. She was a good, relaxed swimmer, / as if she belonged to the bay.

(JOURNALS leaves desk, joining rest of cast in their ac-
tivity: picking up a new notebook and finding his way to
onstage mike.)

LOVE *(begin after "swimmer")*
It was like a chain of broken-circuit Christmas lights. I
loved Marissa for the way she loved her brother. I loved
my son Forrest / for the way he loved his mom.

ADVENTURE *(begin after "Forrest")*
I get the ten dollars and I walk. I walk over the Williamsburg bridge back to the city / feeling triumphant.

CAREER *(begin after "city")*
Please get Spalding Gray's father a copy of *Swimming to
Cambodia*, will you please?

LOVE
Oh the blessed weight of a child, of this child.

JOURNALS
Theo used to come to me and say "Dad, tell me a scary
story" and I who am really not very good at making up stories, said "Look around you. This is the scary story."

But what I don't add and should / is that it is also a story
about wonder and boredom and self-pity, dreck, transcen-
dence and love.

(JOURNALS voice remains foreground with other voices
quieter behind until JOURNALS finishes, then building

to full-throated joy of initial telling of stories earlier in the piece. Each performer again enjoying telling these stories to the audience.)

LOVE *(begin after "should")*
Then we got into dry humping in the field behind Julie's house in September in the sun. I always liked it in the sun. I was happy, / I thought she was happy too.

FAMILY *(begin after "I was happy")*
As I relaxed, I became all body wrapped in a transparent cocoon / of rushing water. Exhausted by the hike and washed clean by the stream, I realized something mattered to me. It was the sharing of all this, of the true story of some of the things that happened to me while living on this earth.

ADVENTURE *(begin after "cocoon")*
It comes around to me and I say, "O Great Spirit, this is Spalding speaking. / And I want to give away the fear I'm about to have a heart attack / at this very moment."

CAREER *(begin after "Spalding speaking")*
And in the play I say, "And they stay here while the earth part of the burns away, burns out. They're waiting / for something they feel is coming. Something important and great."

LOVER *(as ADVENTURE finishes "heart attack")*

She throws her naked body against him saying, "GET BACK LAME DEER GET BACK! GET BACK LAME DEER GET BACK!"

ADVENTURE *(begin after CAREER says "They're waiting." ADVENTURE's last line, "I was happy, etc.," should end overlapping section)*

I would come in my jeans and then we would go and have vanilla Cokes. I was happy and I thought she was happy too.

(All look at FAMILY, listening to the story as they have listened to each other throughout the piece.)

FAMILY

Then Forrest started talking about carpenter ants and how they're so lucky because they live in the thing they eat. "The ants live in the wood and eat it," he said, "I wish I could live in what I eat." And I said, "Well, what would you live in?" and he said, "blue Jello."

(All return to positions they were in during first story, when LOVE read about breakfast.)

LOVE

Now the dinner table is two people calmer. The overhead light is low and the table is lit by two candles. It's all very soft and romantic. Theo seems happy with his baby food and some handfuls of white rice. Kathie and I begin to unwind. We both have some more Chardonnay and I at last begin to feel the wine relaxing me, and easing me down.

Marissa and Forrest have gone out into the living room to play in front of the fire. If either of them is in the mood, they might put a CD on our little Bose in the corner.

If Marissa wins out, as she usually does, it will be Spice Girls, but if Forrest wins, or rather, if Marissa gives over, we will hear Hanson. We hear neither. As Kathie and I sit there in the dining room sipping our wine, we hear a strange new theme emanating from the living room. Kathie cries out, "Oh wow! It's Chumbawamba."

Kathie and I can't resist.

(Chumbawamba's Tubthumper song begins to play softly under the rest of the story.)

She grabs baby Theo out of the highchair and we go into the living room to join Forrest and Marissa in their dance to Chumbawamba. The whole room is filled with a great variety of moves. Marissa is doing balletic leaps across the living room.

Forrest is spinning. I take Theo from Kathie's arms and leave her walking like an Egyptian while I spin Theo around and dance with him. The fire in the fireplace is still burning well and the whole family is dancing. The whole family is dancing to Chumbawamba.

(Chumbawamba's song goes to full volume as story ends. Video of Spalding dancing with yellow tape recorder [from his performance of "Morning, Noon and Night," plays on backdrop as stage goes quickly to black. After about twenty-five seconds of dancing, lights come up fading Spalding's video image to white. Still image of Spalding projects behind performers during bow. Chumbawamba plays throughout bow and continues as audience exits.)

END

DIRECTOR'S NOTES